# MAP OF BENICIA

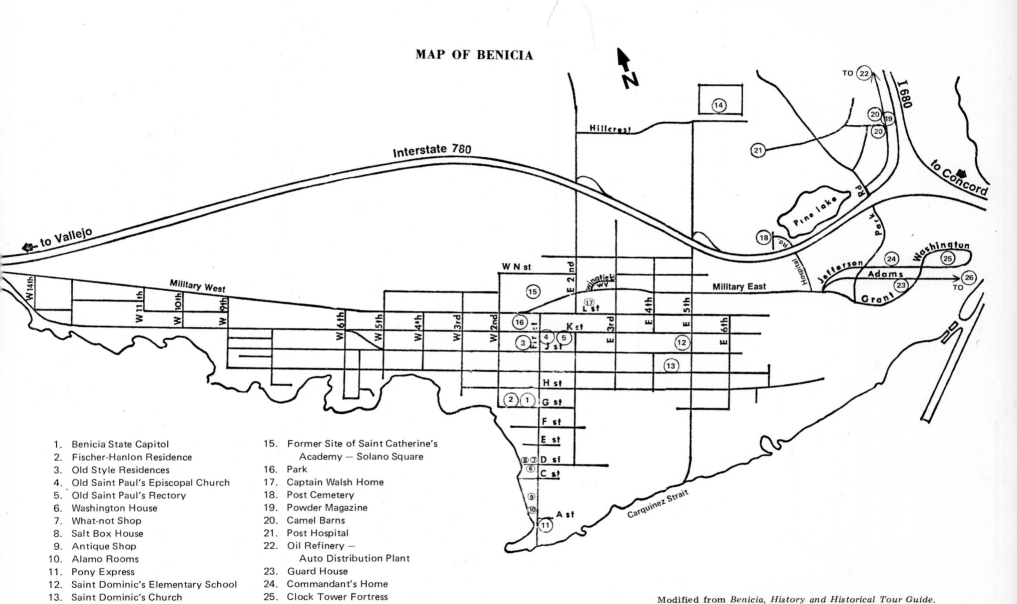

1. Benicia State Capitol
2. Fischer-Hanlon Residence
3. Old Style Residences
4. Old Saint Paul's Episcopal Church
5. Old Saint Paul's Rectory
6. Washington House
7. What-not Shop
8. Salt Box House
9. Antique Shop
10. Alamo Rooms
11. Pony Express
12. Saint Dominic's Elementary School
13. Saint Dominic's Church
14. Saint Dominic's Cemetery

15. Former Site of Saint Catherine's Academy — Solano Square
16. Park
17. Captain Walsh Home
18. Post Cemetery
19. Powder Magazine
20. Camel Barns
21. Post Hospital
22. Oil Refinery — Auto Distribution Plant
23. Guard House
24. Commandant's Home
25. Clock Tower Fortress
26. Port of Benicia

Modified from *Benicia, History and Historical Tour Guide.*
Courtesy, Benicia Chamber of Commerce.

# BENICIA

## WHERE THE PAST MEETS THE PRESENT

# BENICIA

## WHERE THE PAST MEETS THE PRESENT

*By*

**WILLIAM BROOKS DUBLIN**

**WARREN H. GREEN, INC.**

St. Louis, Missouri, U.S.A.

*Published by*

WARREN H. GREEN, INC.
8356 Olive Boulevard
Saint Louis, Missouri 63132

© 1980 by WARREN H. GREEN, INC.

ISBN Number 87527-253-3

*Printed in the United States of America*

# *Preface*

Recently, I had occasion to visit the historic sites of Benicia. It occurred to me that I should share my experience with others, through the medium of photography. It is far from my purpose to replace, or compete with, in any way, the established travel aids, especially the *History and Historical Tour Guide* produced by the Benicia Chamber of Commerce, without which, indeed, it would not have been possible for me to gain my present acquaintance with the points of historical interest of the city. I have drawn freely on the *Tour Guide* for historical orientation, and wish herewith to acknowledge a commensurate debt. The same is true also of the pamphlet *Benicia Capitol State Historic Park,* produced by the Resources Agency of California Department of Parks and Recreation.

It is, rather, my intent simply to present an account of my experience in searching out the points of historical interest in Benicia, as a background for presentation of the photographs which I made.

It may be hoped that some who may not pass through Benicia may yet be interested in seeing photographs of some items of the "old city," and of the new.

It is the people who leave the record, whether this be in the form of edifices, works of art, writings, musical scores, laws, or any of the other varieties of tangible artifacts; accordingly, I have recorded the likenesses of some persons representative of present effort — where the past now meets the present.

I owe a debt of gratitude to so many people of Benicia, who invariably have been courteous and helpful, that I could not remember them all properly. In particular, however, I appreciate the special services rendered by the City Department of Parks and Recreation, and even by the Fire Department (see later). And the Chamber of Commerce staff members have most generously provided information, friendly interest, and warm encouragement of the present project.

W.B.D.

ERRATA

Errors in setting type, that eluded the vigilance of publisher and author: (sorry!)
Page 6, line 6; p. 12, l. 4; p. 32, l. 3:
Capitol should read capital.
Page 52: 1949 of course is 1849.

# List of Photographs

# BENICIA

## WHERE THE PAST MEETS THE PRESENT

Not long ago, I was in the East San Francisco Bay region, driving north along highway 680 from Walnut Creek to Vallejo. I passed over the Benicia-Martinez (George Miller, Jr. Memorial) Bridge that spans the Carquinez Strait. Just below, on the right, I could see the towers of the railroad bridge. Ahead on the right, where the bay widens, the ships of the "fleet in moth balls" were at anchor, standing in rows at attention, waiting patiently for a call to duty. More directly ahead, an automobile distribution unit and the columns and tanks of an oil refinery appeared.

I went through the toll plaza and took the left fork of the dividing road, entering highway 780. Suddenly, there appeared a California Historical Landmark sign, indicating the roadside accessibility of the Benicia State Capitol.

I had long since resolved to become better acquainted with the points of historical interest throughout the state. My mission in Vallejo not being crucially urgent, I obeyed an impulse, and took the next off ramp. Following the historical landmark signs, I found myself driving down First Street, the main thoroughfare of the city, along which buildings of the business section were arranged.

The city was laid out in 1847 according to a simple and effective plan. First Street runs from the waterfront up to the base of a hill; it veers approximately thirty degrees eastward of a true northerly direction. East and West Second, Third, etc. Streets parallel First Street, arranged in series on the appropriate sides. The crossroads are named after the letters of the alphabet, an exception being a main artery, "Military" (no further specification), that crosses at the top of First Street.

## *Benicia State Capitol, with Chief Ranger*

Presently, the early Benicia Capitol appeared on the right (see cover). I turned into G Street, parked and went inside. I entered a foyer leading ahead to a main meeting hall, and on each side giving access to smaller conference rooms. I was received cordially and attended competently by Chief Ranger (it became apparent that the early capitol is a State Park) James Phillips (he appears on the porch in the photograph), who, with his staff, spared no effort to be of assistance.

*five*

## *Dona Benicia Vallejo*

I found, first of all, that Benicia was named for Dona Francesca Filipa Benicia Camilla Vallejo, wife of the general. Her likeness hangs in one of the side rooms.

The early Capitol was completed in 1852 for use as a city hall. It served as the State Capitol for a period of thirteen months during 1853-54 when Benicia was the (third) Capital of the State of California.

## The Senate Chamber

The Senate Chamber, the main meeting room referred to above, is shown in the photograph. (A similar room for the Assembly is on the second floor.) The two desks nearest the opening in the rail are original.

In those days, when the chewing of tobacco was widely practiced, chomping jaws and bulging cheeks made a fine spectacle, and the moist percussion of spitting and the musical *tang* of the spittoons similarly colored the atmosphere. Smoking was not permitted within the building—one had to chew tobacco or take snuff, or go outside to smoke. Unfortunately, we may not credit those concerned with medical preventive foresight; the rule was established to protect the building from the hazard of fire (the rule still holds), without particular care for the lungs involved.

## *Rear of the Senate Chamber*

In the rear of the senate chamber, outside the railing, benches provided seating for a few visitors.

## Press of the Great Seal

In the side rooms, a fine collection of memorabilia is displayed. One of the items is the early press of the Great Seal of the State of California. The seal itself is in Sacramento. On one occasion, persons from Santa Rosa stole the seal, hoping thereby to compel the selection of that city as the capital, but to no avail.

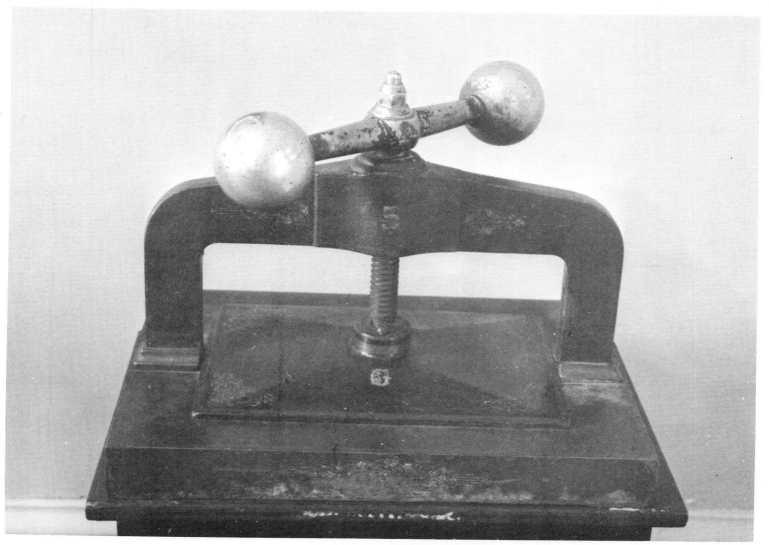

## *Duplicating Press*

The exhibited articles also include a forerunner of the photocopiers of today. It employed a press together with water-soluble ink and the moistening of the paper. As many as six to eight copies could be made from an original.

The Benicia Capitol today serves the most worth-while purpose of education, helping Californians to know their roots.

## *Fischer-Hanlon Residence*

While visiting the Benicia Capitol, I discovered the Fischer-Hanlon House. This handsome residential structure was once a hotel on First Street. In 1856, it was purchased by a Swiss-born Benicia merchant, Joseph Fischer, and was moved to its present location next to the Benicia Capitol, with additions and renovations. The house was occupied by descendants of the Fischer family until 1969, when, with its contents, it was generously given to the State of California, and the Fischer-Hanlon Residence joined the Early Capitol as a part of the State Historical Park. The Residence is cared for by the Docents, an auxiliary body (representative of the historical interest and public-spirited character of Benicia residents) whose members conduct tours through the Residence.

*fifteen*

## A bedroom of the Fischer-Hanlon Residence

The furnishings of the residence reflect the early period of its occupancy.
This is illustrated with a view of one of the bedrooms.

*seventeen*

## *Steinway Piano*

An item of particular interest in the Fischer-Hanlon Residence is a piano, one of three of a kind made by Steinway and shipped to San Francisco in 1869. This piano is the only one of the three that survives.

## *Cook Stove*

In the Residence, cooking was done on a wood-burning stove.

My visit to the Benicia Capitol was productive further in that I was introduced to a pamphlet, *BENICIA — History and Historical Tour Guide,* produced by the Chamber of Commerce. This brought up the reminder that there were other points of interest to the visitor in Old Benicia, marked as such (thirty-nine of them) by the city, and the addresses given in the brochure, and I set out to find them.

It became apparent that many of the original structures no longer exist, and the corresponding points of interest are listed now, and marked, only as sites. But the remainder, still extant, invited exploration.

I found that Old Benicia lies mainly between the foot of First Street, at the bay shore point (the shape of the shore line is somewhat like that of the southern tip of South America) and Military, and between East and West Sixth Streets. The lettered cross streets correspondingly become increasingly short as one progresses down toward A Street, at the shore point.

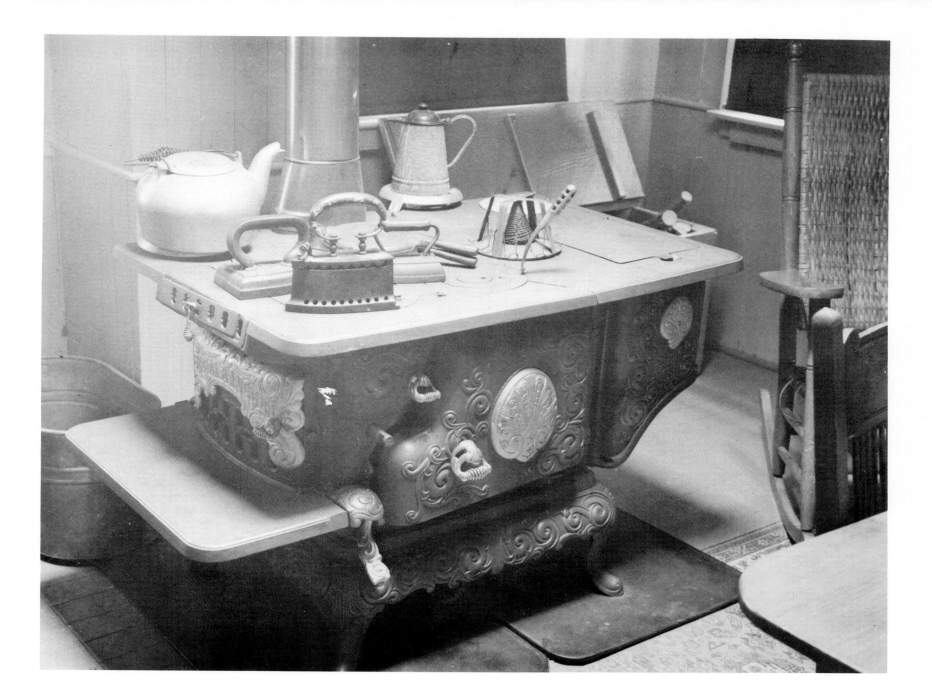

## *Old Style Dwellings*

I had parked near the Old Capitol on G Street, heading west. As I continued along the latter street, I observed several charming dwellings, obviously of early construction. I found more of them on the other cross streets just west of First Street; the houses shown in the photograph are on J Street. The quaintly attractive architectural style of the old houses appears to rest mainly on ornate trim and railings. This appearance contrasts with the more plain-finished character of houses of more recent origin.

*twenty-three*

## Old Saint Paul's Episcopal Church

While I was driving down First Street to locate the early Capitol, I noticed a charming church edifice at the corner of J Street. I turned my attention to this beautiful and historically significant structure.

Old Saint Paul's was built in 1854, the first Episcopal cathedral for Northern California. Work was done by Scandinavian shipwrights from the Pacific Mail and Steamship Company (which see, later). The nautical heritage of the workmen is reflected in the structure of the interior of the church. With its arching beams, the ceiling resembles an inverted ship's hull, and is similar in design to that of Norwegian stave churches. California redwood and wooden dowels were employed.

**Old St. Paul's Sanctuary**

**Old Saint Paul's Nave**

## *Old Saint Paul's Rectory*

The Rectory is next door. It is a typical New England "salt box" type home, built in 1790 in Torrington, Connecticut. It was purchased by Captain Julian McAllister in 1864 (see Clock Tower Fortress, below) and was dismantled and shipped around the horn and reassembled at its present location. Several Benicia houses of this type were so treated.

## *Old St. Paul's — Pastor and Congregation*

Old Saint Paul's is a part of Benicia where the past truly meets the present. I returned the following Sunday morning to attend service. The rector proved to be the Reverend Charles Eldon Davis, Dr. Phil., a most genial and helpful person. He delivered an outstandingly scholarly sermon that nevertheless went to the heart of the problems of living. The scripture centered around the greatest law—love and forgiveness for one's neighbor. I found it interesting and heart-warming that the congregation, as shown in the photograph, where Father Davis is greeting members of the congregation following the service, was of mixed ages. And among four children serving as altar assistants, three races (blonde Caucasian, Oriental, and Black) were represented. The small but dedicated choir similarly showed a mixture of ages and races. Surely, the corner block on which Old Saint Paul's stands is a fortress of American democracy and of spiritual hope for the future.

## *Washington House*

I continued down First Street toward the shore line. At D Street, I found Washington House. This was built in 1850. It housed some members of the state legislature during the period when Benicia was the Capital. In its colorful history, Washington House has served as a hotel, a Chinese lottery, a speakeasy during prohibition days, a bordello, an artist's studio, and now as an antique shop and restaurant.

*thirty-three*

## *What-not Shop*

Nearby on D Street West, which amounts to no more than a short block, I found two structures marked by the city. One of these was the What-not Shop. This structure was among the earliest in Benicia. It was prefabricated in Maine, and was shipped and reassembled at its present location approximately in 1848.

*thirty-five*

## *Salt Box House*

The other item on D Street was the Salt Box House. This structure, again, was prefabricated on the East coast and shipped in sections to California to be reassembled, during gold rush days. It is now a private residence. The house is a simple, small box, just as it is named (see also the St. Paul's Rectory, earlier).

## *Antique Shop*

There are several antique shops on First Street. The buildings tend to show the early architectural trim. An example is shown in the photograph.

## The Alamo Rooms

Another building of interest was found a short added distance down First Street. Built in 1868, serving as a private residence, then as a rooming house and restaurant for railroad men, The "Alamo Rooms" was a brothel during the 1940's and early 1950's. An upstairs room was provided with an invisible door for quick hiding. Today, the building houses a restaurant; an antique shop occupies the upstairs.

*thirty-nine*

## *Pony Express*

Benicia was a vital link in the Pony Express system. On seeing an automobile drive up and pull away, after first disbelief and alarm, respectively, riders and their mounts would doubtless have felt insecure in their positions, and this would have been heightened on seeing an airplane pass overhead (note the vapor trail). It was the advent of the telegraph, however, in 1861, that brought an end to the Pony Express. The station, shown in the photograph, is at the foot of First Street, on the shore of the "point," at A Street; the latter scarcely extends past the station.

## Saint Catherine's Academy and Convent

The Congregation of the Dominican Sisters of San Rafael was founded by Mother Mary Goemaere, a French nun whose journey to California included crossing the Isthmus of Panama, in part by canoe up the Chagres River, the remainder by mule-back. The order was established in 1851 in Monterey, moving to Benicia in 1854. (In time, the Mother House was established in San Rafael.) The sisters shared the general expectation that Benicia would become the metropolis of Northern California, situated as it was at the head of ocean navigation and being in a position to command the trade of the interior rivers and valleys. Saint Catherine's Academy and Convent was built where the Solano Square business, professional and shopping center now stands (which see, later). The amount of good done by the Dominican Sisters in California, extending from early days into the present, has been and still is, incalculable.

ST. CATHERINE'S CONVENT, BENICIA, CAL.

*forty-three*

*Principal of Saint Dominic's Elementary School,*

*with statue of the patron saint*

The work of the sisters expanded so that they now conduct several hospitals and schools, and a college. These include an elementary school in Benicia. In the photograph, the principal, Sister Leona, stands at the school entrance, by a statue of the patron saint. Sister Leona informed me that the Franciscan order would take over the running of the school sometime during the ensuing year.

## *Saint Dominic's Church*

Saint Dominic's Church was built in 1852 by the Dominican Fathers. I located it by retracing my way to I Street and driving to the block between Fourth and Fifth Streets, East.

*forty-seven*

# *Saint Dominic's Cemetery*

Saint Dominic's Cemetery is a point of interest listed in the tour guide. Since I was near East Fifth Street (Second and Fifth Streets, East appear to be the main thoroughfares extending up over the hill), I drove north over it, under the freeway, up on the hill, to Hillcrest Avenue, where I found the cemetery, situated between East Fifth and Sixth Streets. There appeared to be two differing sections, one for the members of the order, and one for the laity. The graves of the fathers and those of the sisters are segregated. Those of the sisters are on the left as one enters the cemetery. The headstones are of simple type, like those of the military (which see, below). The grave of Sister Mary Dominica Arguello lies at the right hand margin of the front row, as shown in the photograph. Cut flowers had been placed at the grave. Sister Mary was betrothed to the Russian Count Nicholai Resanov. He died accidently during a trip to Russia to obtain the consent of the Czar to marry. Many years later (when past the age of sixty), Sister Mary, still faithful to her love, learned of the tragedy. She then became the first native daughter to be admitted to the order.

Leaving Saint Dominic's Cemetery, I drove west to West Second Street and passed down the hill and under the freeway, retracing the route taken when searching for the early Capitol. At First Street and Military, I found Solano Square, a thriving business, professional and shopping complex, occupying the site where Saint Catherine's Academy and Convent once stood. On the far corner to the left was the park, in which a bandstand occupied a prominent position. One could hear the ghostly strains of *Seeing Nellie Home* and *You were Sixteen,* probably with one or two instruments a little out of tune, providing local color. On hearing some of today's offerings, the horses would doubtless have torn loose from the hitching rail and gone whinnying madly down the street.

*Solano Square*

*The Park*

## Captain Walsh Home

I turned left (east) on L Street. On the right there appeared the city administrative complex. On the left, across from City Hall, and just past Second Street, I found another marked point of interest: the Captain Walsh Home. John Walsh, a retired sailing vessel captain, settled in Benicia in 1849. His home was one of three identical houses shipped around the Horn from Boston. The home is now a private residence.

## Post Cemetery

I passed to Military and proceeded eastward. The Post Cemetery is a point of interest marked by the city and listed in the tour guide. In order to reach it, one turns left from Military, up Hospital Road, just before entering the gate of Industrial Park. Passing up a rise, through a fence gate, and under the pipeline, I found the entrance. The gates are open daily from 8:30 A.M. to 4:30 P.M.

The Old Post Cemetery was formerly a part of the Benicia Arsenal, whose grounds now house the Industrial Park; Benicia was a center for defense.

The cemetery is well-kept. Its availability to visitors is highlighted by a city marking sign and an explanatory placard posted in the parking area. Gravestones date from the mid 1840's to the World War II period. Some are not dated. In addition to those of servicemen, remains include some of family members. Some headstones are marked: "Unknown Soldier," "Unknown Civilian," and in some cases, simply "Unknown." A few dogs are buried in the cemetery—their headstones are missing owing to vandalism, said to be a problem. The remains of eight German prisoners of war lie apart from the American. Remains of Italian prisoners appear to have been returned to the homeland, although one private appears to have been overlooked—at any rate, one such grave (the only Italian one that I found) is in the main, American section. Where visible, names have been masked out to ensure privacy.

Although the day was not a special one, flowers were observed at some of the headstones. In one such case, the inscription included: ". . . . 1893, age 19." A respectable ceremonial program was conducted last Memorial Day.

*Post Cemetery —*

*Graves of Foreign Soldiers*

I returned to Military and continued east. On reaching a fork, I bore left, on Adams Street. At Park Road, I turned up to the left, over a hill, and passing a car distribution plant on the right, I went under the freeway. The first turn to the right, onto an unmarked street, was explored with success. Passing a toy-producing establishment on the left, I found myself on a narrow black-top road flanked on each side by a field covered with a solid growth of tall weeds.

## *Powder Magazine*

I soon approached a crossroad. Turning down to the right, I found the Powder Magazine of the old arsenal. This structure, built of sandstone hewn from the surrounding hills, is said to be one of California's finest examples of the stonecutter's art. French craftsmen were brought to the Arsenal especial-ly for the construction of this and some other sandstone buildings (i.e., see Camel Barns, later) which became the Arsenal's first permanent structures.

## *Interior of Powder Magazine*

The walls are of four-foot-thick solid stone. The ceiling is vaulted, and the interior Corinthian columns are hand-carved. So that the reader of this account could see the interior of the magazine (the latter not ordinarily being open to visitors), representatives of the City Department of Parks and Recreation kindly opened the door, and firefighters from the nearby station set up flood lights.

Returning to the black-top road, I continued ahead, and soon approached an oil refinery, with an automobile distribution center below and on the right, across freeway and railroad tracks. These units appear situated convenient to rail and truck transportation.

*Oil Refinery*

*Auto Distribution Plant*

## *Camel Barns*

I returned to the crossroad leading to the Powder Magazine, and turning the other way, reached the Camel Barns, which could be seen from the crossroad. These buildings appear to show the fine stone masonry exhibited by the Powder Magazine. Built originally to serve as warehouses, the barns were used for a time for stabling a herd of camels imported in 1856 as an experiment in transportation of supplies across the southwestern desert. The camels were sold at auction in 1864. The last of them died in Griffith Park, Los Angeles, in 1934. (It is a small world; I saw the camels during a visit to the zoo in the late twenties!)

## Inside of one of the Camel Barns —
## Otis Elevator

The barn on reader's left in the photograph shows no sign of activity. The one on the right is used by a firm manufacturing wallpaper. Among the facilities is one of the first Otis elevators, shown in the photograph, still in service. It rides on wooden runners.

## Post Hospital

Another listed point of interest is the old Post Hospital. Leaving the Camel Barns and continuing in the same direction as previously (i.e., away from the Powder Magazine), I passed uphill to rejoin Park Road. Turning to the right, I continued ahead until the large yellow Exxon pipeline appeared on the left, and storage tanks on the right. Having just passed the end of a fenced-in parking lot, I took the first turn to the left, on an unmarked road, and taking a short stretch of road branching off to the right, and passing uphill, I approached the Post Hospital.

This structure, built in 1856, was the first military hospital in the West. It also was constructed of sandstone blocks. It served in the care of wounded servicemen from as far away as the Northwest Territory (if the patient could survive the trip, his chances of making it out of the hospital must have been fairly good). The hospital continued in service through the various wars including the Korean conflict. (One wonders what proportion of medical care could have been provided in a facility of that size, compared with that of the governmental hospitals available concurrently.) During World War II, the building served as the Post Chapel (note the belfry, in the photograph). At the time of my visit, there was no sign of activity within the building; workmen from a nearby plant used the porch (offering shade) and steps for lounging and eating during lunch and other free periods (note the waste can). The grounds served for car parking.

## *Guard House*

I returned over Park Road to Adams Street and continued east along that thoroughfare. I passed the previously mentioned fire station, and came to the Guard House. This was the third guardhouse (1872) built on the Benicia Arsenal grounds. The first of such buildings, constructed in 1852, and not now in evidence, provided temporary quarters for Ulysses S. Grant when he was tried and found guilty of a minor infraction of military regulations.

## *Commandant's Home*

Continuing along Adams Street, I encountered a sign directing one uphill to the left, on an unmarked street, to the Commandant's Home. This structure came in view on the left, on the hill. Built in 1860, the Home is a twenty-room mansion of classic Georgian design, with fourteen-foot ceilings and twenty-four-inch-thick brick walls. The Home served as center for many social functions of the elite Bay Area society in the latter half of the nineteenth century. Today, the residence is in active service as a restaurant. (So far as I could see, I was the only visitor who came just to observe—the others, of whom there were plenty, their cars filling the parking space, were there to eat.)

## Clock Tower Fortress — Tower Wall

On the other, right hand side of the street was the approach to the Clock Tower Fortress. This structure was the first U. S. Military bastion and storehouse constructed (1859) in California. It was built to command Carquinez Strait and to protect the post from Indian attacks that never came. The walls are of two-foot-thick sandstone. One photograph shows the tower wall (and one side); the other, the opposite wall overlooking the Strait. The large Seth Thomas clock was installed as a memorial to Colonel Julian McAllister, who commanded the Arsenal for twenty-five years. (We have met him before, as purchaser of the Saint Paul's Rectory, when he was a captain [which see, above].) The Fortress is in active use (reminiscent of the well-preserved British castles) — the upper level serves as the community's activity center, while the lower level may be used by the Benicia Historical Society. One is tempted to raise the question of *snafu* when we are told that the narrow slots seen along the longer walls, or sides, were for rifle practice, while the larger openings seen in the ends, or shorter walls, were for cannon fire!

*Clock Tower Fortress —*

*The Wall Overlooking the Strait*

## Port of Benicia

I returned downhill to Adams Street. Continuing ahead, I entered a fence gate and proceeded downhill to the waterfront. The Port of Benicia has always been an important business function of the community. In 1850, the Pacific Mail and Steamship Company was the first large industrial enterprise in California, and Benicia became an active center for shipping. (See above, role of workmen from the company in the building of Old Saint Paul's.) Today, the port activities emphasize the receipt of oil for the refinery. Of the three photographs of the dock, the first is one of the tanker Benicia, a very large ship just qualifying (I was informed), at 165,000 tons, as a super-tanker, this class ranging from 160,000 to 300,000 tons. A ship nearly twice the size of the Benicia would be truly gigantic. The Benicia is shown tied at the Exxon pipeline. The latter, which I encountered several times during my tour through the Industrial Park district, winds like a giant serpent toward its point of delivery at the refinery. In the second photograph, a ship is shown tied at a location apparently equipped for the transfer of grain, as the conveyor seen extending to the ship led to a cluster of silos. The third photograph was made (on another day) from the overlooking hill, near the point at which the seaward wall of the Fortress was photographed. It shows the Exxon Galveston, a tanker somewhat smaller than the Benicia. It also is hooked to the pipeline. The bridge over the strait is seen on the left, and in the background, on the Martinez side of the strait, where a still larger complex of refineries operates, an Arco tanker is tied.

One refrains with difficulty from philosophizing when the subject of oil is introduced. But that is another story.

*Port of Benicia*

*Port of Benicia*

*Port of Benicia*

# DATE DUE